FOOTBALL WORLD CUP

Clive Gifford

First published in Great Britain in 2009 by ticktock Media Ltd,
The Old Sawmill, 103 Goods Station Road, Tunbridge Wells, Kent, TN1 2DP

project editor and picture researcher: Ruth Owen
ticktock project designer: Simon Fenn

Thank you to Lorraine Petersen and the members of **nasen**

ISBN 978 1 84696 947 8 pbk

Printed in China

A CIP catalogue record for this book is available from the British Library.

Picture credits (t=top; b=bottom; c=centre; l=left; r=right):
AFP/Getty Images: 2-3, 5t, 5b, 8-9, 11r, 14, 19, 23, 28-29, 31. Bongarts/Getty Images: 4, 6-7, 22-23 (main). Getty Images: 11l, 13, 15, 16-17, 18, 24-25, 26, 27. Panoramic/Panoramic/PA Photos: 21b. Shutterstock: 1, 10, 12, 20, 21t, 21 (background), 26-27 (background), 30-31 (background). Sipa Press/Rex Features: OFC.

Every effort has been made to trace copyright holders, and we apologise in advance for any omissions. We would be pleased to insert the appropriate acknowledgments in any subsequent edition of this publication.

CONTENTS

THE BIG ONE

The FIFA World Cup is the biggest football competition on Earth.

Every four years, 32 national teams take part in the World Cup finals.

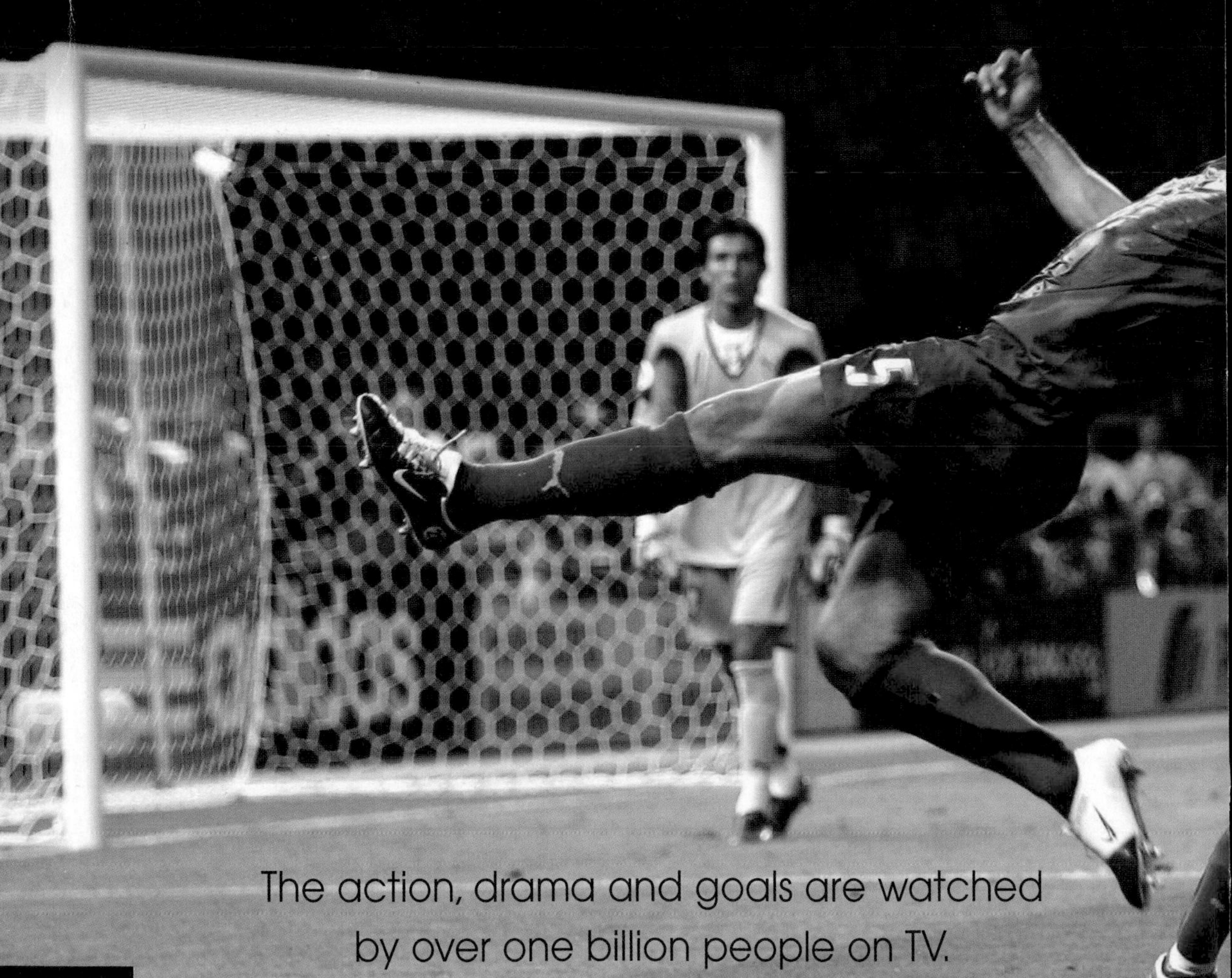

The action, drama and goals are watched by over one billion people on TV.

The 2006 World Cup Final between Italy and France.

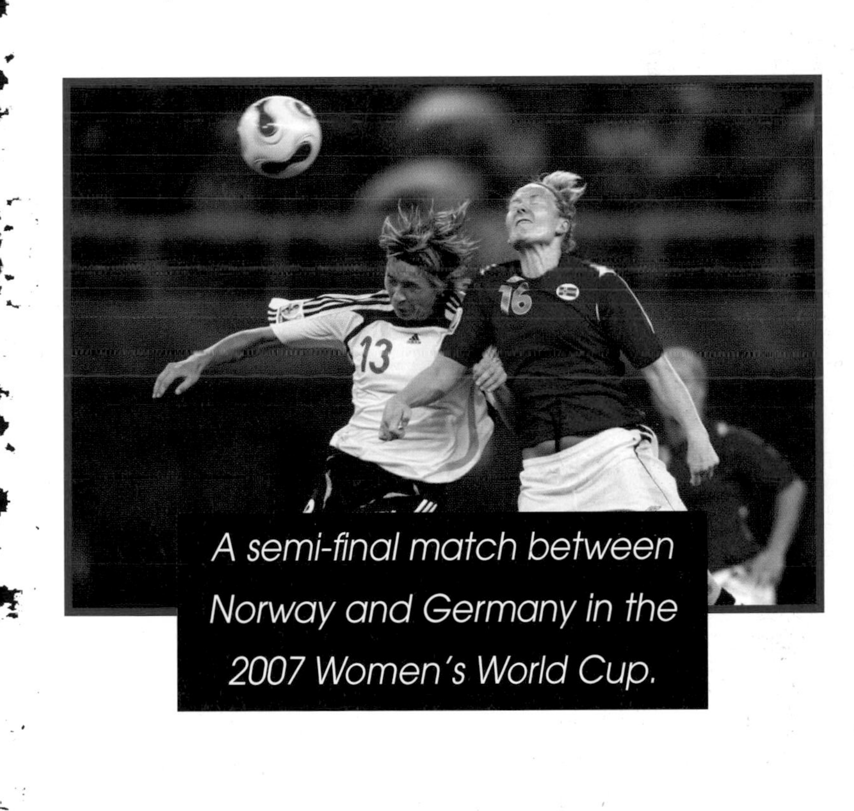

A semi-final match between Norway and Germany in the 2007 Women's World Cup.

Only seven teams have ever won the World Cup.

THE ULTIMATE PRIZE

This is it! The ultimate prize – the FIFA World Cup Trophy. The trophy is made of gold.

The first World Cup trophy was called the "Jules Rimet Cup". It had an eventful life.

During World War II, the cup was hidden in a shoebox under the bed of an Italian football official. This was to stop it from being stolen by German soldiers.

In 1966, the cup was stolen just before the tournament. A small dog named Pickles found it buried under a tree!

When Brazil won the cup for the third time, they were allowed to keep it. But in 1983 it was stolen. The thieves melted it down for the gold.

Today, the winning team only gets a copy of the FIFA World Cup Trophy. They do not get the real gold one!

HOSTS

FIFA chooses which country will host a World Cup tournament. Being the host is a big deal.

New stadiums have to be built.

Several million football fans need a way to get to and from the games. They also need food and places to stay. Extra police are needed to keep things running smoothly.

FUTURE HOSTS

In 2010, South Africa will host the World Cup finals. In 2014, it will be Brazil.

This is the International Stadium Yokohama in Japan. In 2002, 69,000 fans packed the stadium for the World Cup Final match between Germany and Brazil.

WORLD CUP FEVER

Fans flock to the World Cup finals. They want to watch their football heroes in action.

The most fans that ever crammed into one stadium was 199,854. The event was the 1950 World Cup Final match between Brazil and Uruguay. The match was played in the Maracana Stadium in Brazil.

ATTENDANCE NUMBERS

Year	Host Country	FIFA Total Attendance
2006	Germany	3,359,439
2002	Korea/Japan	2,705,197
1998	France	2,785,100
1994	USA	3,587,538
1990	Italy	2,516,348

At the 2002 World Cup finals, Japanese player Tsuneyasu Miyamoto wore a mask. He wore it to protect his face.

Thousands of Japanese fans copied their favourite player.

GETTING TO THE FINALS

Over 200 countries try to get their teams into the World Cup finals.

Teams play matches called qualifiers.

If a team wins enough matches, it will be one of the 32 teams to play in the finals.

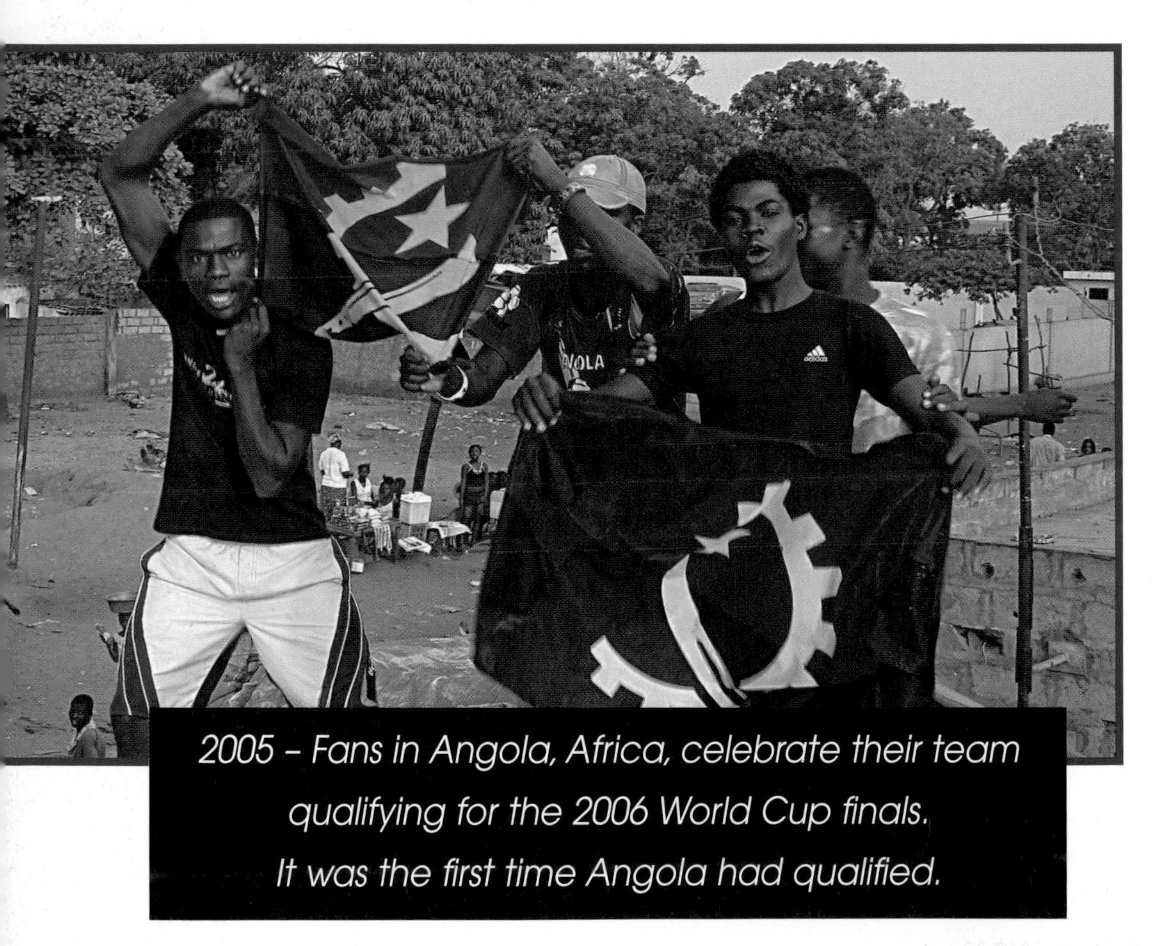

2005 – Fans in Angola, Africa, celebrate their team qualifying for the 2006 World Cup finals. It was the first time Angola had qualified.

Miss out on qualifying, and it's heartbreak!

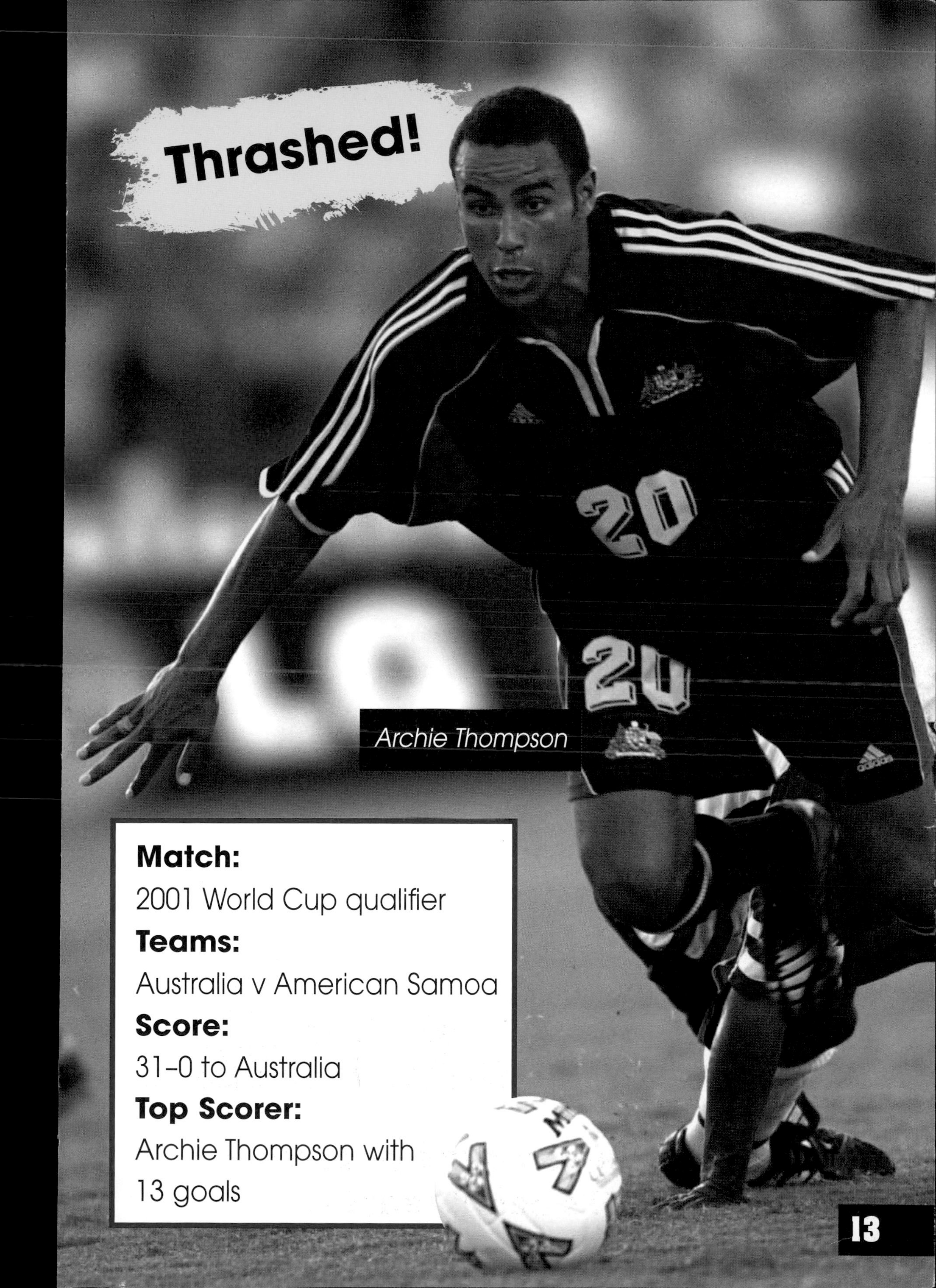

Thrashed!

Archie Thompson

Match:

2001 World Cup qualifier

Teams:

Australia v American Samoa

Score:

31–0 to Australia

Top Scorer:

Archie Thompson with 13 goals

THE TOURNAMENT

Six tough games stand between a team and a World Cup Final.

Months before the tournament starts, the "group draw" is made at a special event.

A group is drawn for the 2006 World Cup final.

The 32 final teams are drawn at random and placed in groups of four. The four teams in each group will all play each other. The top two teams from each group go on to play in the "round of 16".

Games are now knockout. The pressure is really on.

The 16 teams play in eight matches. The eight winning teams go through to the quarter finals. The losing teams go home.

1998 – France celebrate winning their quarter finals game against Italy.

The winners of the quarter finals go through to the semi-finals.

SHOOT-OUTS

In the knockout rounds of the tournament, a game cannot end with a draw.

If the game is level at the end, 30 minutes of extra time is played. If the score is still level after extra time, it's penalty shoot-out time!

Teams take turns to take a penalty. Each team shoots five penalties.

The team who scores the most wins.

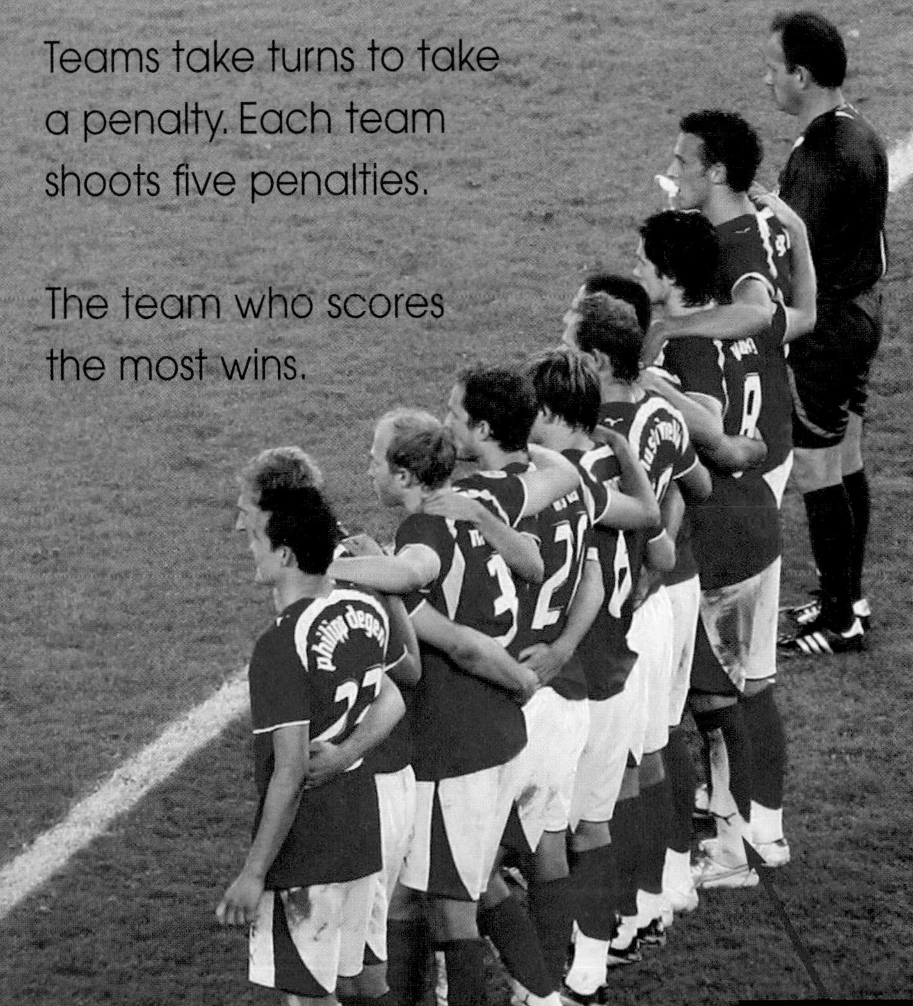

2006 – Heartbreak for Switzerland.

2006 – Joy for Ukraine as they knock out Switzerland in a penalty shoot-out.

If the scores are still level after five penalties each, the teams carry on until one team misses!

There have been 20 penalty shoot-outs in World Cup finals.

WINNERS

There have been 18 World Cup tournaments. Only seven teams have won the World Cup.

Six World Cups have been won by the team hosting the tournament.

WORLD CUP WINNERS

- Brazil – 5 times
- Italy – 4 times
- Germany – 3 times
- Argentina – twice
- Uruguay – twice
- England – once
- France – once

1966 – England beat Germany in the World Cup Final held in London, England.

> To hold the World Cup in my hands is one of the most incredible moments in my life.
>
> *Brazilian striker Ronaldo*

2002 – Brazil's Ronaldo battles it out against Germany in the World Cup Final.

ALL-TIME GREAT

Only one player has won as a team captain (1974) and later, as a coach (1990). That man is Franz Beckenbauer of Germany.

BRILLIANT BRAZIL

Brazil is the best. No question!
They have won the World Cup five times and reached the semi-finals 10 times.

Brazil is the only team to have qualified and played in every single World Cup.

	Played	Won	Drawn	Lost	Goals Scored
1. Brazil	92	64	14	14	201
2. Germany	92	55	19	18	190
3. Italy	77	44	19	14	122

Brazilian player Pelé is the only three time World Cup winner. He was on the winning team in 1958, 1962 and 1970.

Fans hold pictures of Pelé and Ronaldo.

Brazil's Ronaldo is the top World Cup scorer. He has scored a total of 15 goals in World Cup tournaments.

1970 – Pelé celebrates scoring the first goal in the World Cup Final between Brazil and Italy.

WOMEN'S WORLD CUP

The FIFA Women's World Cup began in 1991. Teams from 16 countries take part.

Germany's 2007 win earned the team over half a million pounds in prize money.

The team didn't let a single goal in during the tournament. In their opening game, Germany beat Argentina 11-0. That's a World Cup record.

2007 – Birgit Prinz of Germany scores her third goal against Argentina.

Two players have appeared at all five Women's World Cups:

- Bente Nordby – Goalkeeper (Norway)
- Kristine Lilly – Midfielder (USA)

Kristine Lilly has played an amazing 340 times for the USA. She has scored 129 goals for her country.

WOMEN'S WORLD CUP WINNERS

- 2007 - Germany
- 2003 - Germany
- 1999 - USA
- 1995 - Norway
- 1991 - USA

WORLD CUP WONDERS

Most Appearances

Lothar Matthäus, Germany	25
Paolo Maldini, Italy	23
Diego Maradona, Argentina	21

Fastest Goals

- Hakan Sükür of Turkey
  11 seconds - 2002

- Vaclav Masek of Czechoslovakia
  15 seconds - 1962

Top Goalscorers

Ronaldo, Brazil	15
Gerd Müller, Germany	14
Juste Fontaine, France	13
Pelé, Brazil	12
Sandor Kocsis, Hungary	11
Jürgen Klinsmann, Germany	11

The most red cards in one match was four. The game was between Portugal and the Netherlands in 2006.

REFEREES

Being a referee is hard. Being a World Cup referee is the toughest.

The whole world is watching.

You don't want to make a mistake...

...like English referee Graham Poll did in 2006.

He showed the yellow card to Josip Simunic of Croatia three times. You should be sent off if you get two yellows.

346 **The most yellow cards at one World Cup in 2006.**

Jean Langenus was the referee at the first World Cup Final in 1930.

He didn't wear black like today's referees. He wore horseriding trousers, a dinner jacket and tie!

142 **The total number of red cards in all World Cups.**

56 **The number of seconds José Batista of Uruguay was on the pitch before he was sent off in 1986.**

SHOCKS!

Shocks happen! That's what's so great about the World Cup.

At the 2002 World Cup, South Korea knocked out favourites, Italy, in the round of 16 stage.

Ahn Jung Hwan scored for South Korea. However, Hwan played for an Italian football club. He was not very popular back in Italy!

2002 – South Korea celebrate their shock win!

At the 1950 World Cup, England was a top team. But the USA beat them 1–0. The USA's goal scorer had a day job. He did the washing up at a restaurant!

Winning Streak

Bulgaria had never won a game in a World Cup tournament.

Then in 1994, Bulgaria beat Greece, Argentina, Mexico and Germany in a row to reach the semi-finals.

GREATEST COMEBACK - 1954

	Switzerland	Austria
At half time	3	0
Final score	5	7

Need to know words

FIFA The organisation that runs world football competitions. FIFA was formed in 1904.

group draw When the 32 teams that reach the World Cup final are put into eight groups of four. The teams are drawn at random at a special event.

host The act of holding and running the World Cup final. Also the word for the country which holds the World Cup final.

mascot A cartoon-like character or object which is a symbol of a football club or of a World Cup tournament.

midfielder A player who plays in the middle of the pitch and is skilled in attack and defence.

penalty A shot at the goal awarded by the referee for a serious foul.

qualifier One of a series of matches played by teams with the aim of getting to the World Cup finals.

quarter finals Four matches played by the last eight teams in a tournament.

red card A card shown by a referee to send a player off the pitch.

semi-finals Two matches played by the last four teams in a tournament. The two winning teams play each other in the final.

stadium The building which holds a football pitch and seats for thousands of spectators.

yellow card A card shown by a referee to a player as a warning.

MASCOT MANIA

The first World Cup mascot appeared in 1966. He was a dog called World Cup Willie.

There have been some strange mascots since then.

- A giant orange in Spain in 1982.
- A chilli pepper wearing a moustache and sombrero hat in Mexico in 1986.
- A lion and talking football in Germany in 2006.

The 2006 mascot Goleo and the talking ball Pille.

WORLD CUP ONLINE

Websites

http://www.fifa.com/worldcup/index.html

http://www.planetworldcup.com/

http://www.fifaworldcup.co.uk/

http://news.bbc.co.uk/sport1/hi/football/world_cup_2006/default.stm

Index